A Look At...

Icy Worlds

WORLD
BOOK

a Scott Fetzer company
Chicago
www.worldbookonline.com

Staff:

Executive Committee

President
Donald D. Keller

Vice President and Editor in Chief
Paul A. Kobasa

Vice President, Marketing/ Digital Products
Sean Klunder

Vice President, International
Richard Flower

Director, Human Resources
Bev Ecker

Editorial

Associate Director, Supplementary Publications
Scott Thomas

Associate Manager, Supplementary Publications
Cassie Mayer

Researcher, Supplementary Publications
Annie Brodsky

Manager, Indexing Services
David Pofelski

Manager, Contracts & Compliance (Rights & Permissions)
Loranne K. Shields

Editorial Administration

Director, Systems and Projects
Tony Tills

Senior Manager, Publishing Operations
Timothy Falk

Associate Manager, Publishing Operations
Audrey Casey

Graphics and Design

Manager
Tom Evans

Manager, Cartographic Services
Wayne K. Pichler

Senior Cartographer
John Rejba

Book Design by
Matt Carrington

Senior Designer
Isaiah Sheppard

Contributing Designer
Lucy Lesiak

Photo Editor
Kathy Creech

Contributing Photo Editor
Clover Morell

Production

Director, Manufacturing and Pre-Press
Carma Fazio

Manufacturing Manager
Steven K. Hueppchen

Production/ Technology Manager
Anne Fritzinger

Proofreader
Emilie Schrage

World Book, Inc.
233 N. Michigan Avenue
Chicago, IL 60601

For information about other World Book publications, visit our website at http://www.worldbookonline.com or call **1-800-WORLDBK (967-5325).**
For information about sales to schools and libraries, call **1-800-975-3250 (United States)**, or **1-800-837-5365 (Canada).**

Library of Congress Cataloging-in-Publication Data
Icy worlds
     p. cm. — (A look at ...)
  Includes index.
  Summary: "An introduction to regions with cold climates, including Earth's polar regions and high-elevation mountain regions, with information about the animals, plants, and people that live there and the explorers who first described these areas. Features include fact boxes, illustrations, period photographs, a glossary, and a list of recommended books and websites"—Provided by publisher.
  ISBN 978-0-7166-1788-4
  1. Polar regions--Juvenile literature. 2. Alpine regions--Juvenile literature. 3. Ice--Juvenile literature. 4. Cold--Juvenile literature. 5. Natural history--Juvenile literature. 6. Explorers--Arctic regions--History--Juvenile literature. I. World Book, Inc.
  G590.I28 2011
  911--dc22
                   2011011517

A Look At ...
Set ISBN 978-0-7166-1786-0

Printed in China by Shenzhen Donnelley Printing Co., Ltd.
Guangdong Province
1st printing July 2011

Picture Acknowledgments:

The publishers gratefully acknowledge the following sources for photography. All illustrations and maps were prepared by WORLD BOOK unless otherwise noted.

Front cover: Shutterstock
Accent Alaska/Alamy Images 52, 53; Alaska Stock/Alamy Images 52; Arcticphoto/Alamy Images 32, 49, 56; Ashley Cooper, Alamy Images 37; Michael DeFreitas, Alamy Images 16; John Elk III, Alamy Images 24; Martin Harvey, Alamy Images 10; INTERFOTO/Alamy Images 23; Michael Jenner, Alamy Images 33; Dan Leeth, Alamy Images 48; Lonely Planet Images/Alamy Images 46; Galen Rowell, Mountain Light/Alamy Images 39, 45; ASP GeoImaging/NASA/Alamy Images 4; Picture Contact BV/Alamy Images 34; Robert Preston, Alamy Images 10; Lee Thomas, Alamy Images 20; Visual & Written SL/Alamy Images 32; Kim Westerskov, Alamy Images 20; AP Images 36, 57; Aristide Economopoulos, Star Ledger/Corbis 58; Hulton-Deutsch Collection/Corbis 42; Dreamstime 6,12, 27, 28, 37, 38; Express Newspapers/Getty Images 45; Sue Flood, Getty Images 40; Hulton Archive/Getty Images 26, 43; Roy Philippe, hemis.fr/Getty Images 8; Harald Sund, Getty Images 16; Doug Allan, The Image Bank/Getty Images 17; Paul Nicklen, National Geographic/Getty Images 31; Radius Images/Getty Images 55; Fred Hirschmann, Science Faction/Getty Images 58; Flip Nicklin, Minden Pictures, 51; NASA 40, 50, 60, 61; Bryan & Cherry Alexander, Photo Researchers 47; Bernhard Edmaier, Photo Researchers, 18; Warren Photographic/Photo Researchers 14; Shutterstock 4, 6, 9, 13, 19, 22, 24, 29, 30, 54, 56, 59; Corbis/SuperStock 21; Minden Pictures/SuperStock 46.

CONTENTS

There is a glossary on page 62. Terms defined in the glossary are in type
that looks like this on their first appearance on any spread (two facing pages).

Introducing Icy Worlds

Earth has many different regions and climates. Some places are cold and ice-covered all the time.

Earth has oceans and continents. Some parts of Earth are usually warm. Others are usually cold. Still other parts experience both warm and cold temperatures.

Earth also has an **atmosphere** (mass of gases) surrounding it. Nearly all of Earth's weather takes place in the lowest layer of the atmosphere. Weather conditions can include temperature, wind, and **precipitation** (forms of water falling from the sky, such as rain or snow).

The kind of weather that occurs at a particular place over a long period is its **climate.** Some places on Earth have a cold climate. Others have a warm or hot climate. Climates in many places consist of cycles of weather that repeat year after year. In these climates, a cool or cold season is followed by a warm or hot season.

This book is about places on Earth that have very cold climates. Such places are covered with ice or snow most or all of the year. They are quite different from other world regions. Earth's icy worlds have much to teach us about our planet, its past, and its future.

A satellite image of Earth shows the ice-covered lands of the Arctic.

How are icy worlds unique?

Cold, icy places differ in many ways from hot places or **temperate regions** (places that experience heat and cold at different times of the year). One obvious difference is the presence of ice and snow year-round. On much of Earth, precipitation falls as rain. Rain hits land and quickly runs off. It often follows the paths of creeks, rivers, and other streams all the way to the sea.

But in very cold places, the precipitation almost always falls as snow or ice. Icy precipitation does not run off the land. It accumulates (piles up). Cold temperatures keep the snow from melting. Over time, the weight of the snow presses down, forming a huge mass of solid ice called a **glacier.**

Measuring Temperature

Fahrenheit (or F) and Celsius (or C) identify different scales for measuring temperature. In the United States, temperatures are often measured in degrees Fahrenheit. However, in most other parts of the world, temperatures are usually measured in degrees Celsius. This table compares temperatures in the two scales.

	Fahrenheit (°F)	Celsius (°C)
Freezing point of water	32°	0°
An unusually hot day	100°	38°
Boiling point of water	212°	100°

Extreme Temperatures

Earth's atmosphere protects our planet from great temperature extremes. Worlds with little or no atmosphere—such as our moon—experience far hotter and colder temperatures.

Coldest temperature recorded on Earth
−128.6 °F (−89.2 °C) at Vostok Station, Antarctica, on July 21, 1983

Hottest temperature recorded on Earth
136 °F (58 °C) at Al Aziziyah, Libya, on September 13, 1922

Coldest temperature on the moon (estimate)
−400 °F (−240 °C) in always-shaded deep craters

Hottest temperature on the moon (estimate)
253 °F (123 °C) on surface exposed to daytime sun

Exploring icy worlds

For centuries, people in warmer climates knew little or nothing about Earth's cold, icy places. Then, several hundred years ago, explorers began to visit and map these regions. Today, most surface regions of the world have been explored and mapped.

Weather **satellites** (human-made objects that circle high above a planet) have greatly expanded our knowledge of icy worlds. These satellites continually photograph weather conditions throughout the world as they orbit Earth.

Some regions of Earth are cold, icy places because of where they lie on the globe. Living things have developed ways to survive in these regions.

Why are there cold, icy regions?

Think of Earth as a big ball facing a bright lamp—the sun. The region of Earth where the sun appears directly overhead in the middle of the day receives strong rays of light. This part of Earth is called the equatorial region because the equator runs through it. Most lands in the equatorial region have hot weather all the time. However, the parts of Earth farthest from the equator receive weaker, indirect rays of sunlight. These parts of Earth are called the polar regions.

In addition, Earth spins on an **axis** that is tilted in relation to the sun instead of straight up-and-down. (An axis is an imaginary line through the center of a ball.) In the different seasons, Earth's axis tilts parts of Earth either toward or away from the sun. For this reason, much of Earth experiences the four seasons of winter, spring, summer, and fall.

In the polar regions, sunlight can disappear altogether for part of the year. Because of the way Earth tilts toward the sun, each polar region receives little or no light for six months of the year. For the other six months, each polar region has some light most or all of the time. However, sunlight in the polar regions is never direct or strong.

The sun heats Earth unevenly, producing cooler **climates** at increasing distances from the equator.

Arctic foxes have long, thick winter fur to protect them from the extreme cold. Their relatively small ears also keep them from losing too much body heat.

People living in polar regions have extremely long nights—or a single night that lasts for months. In Barrow, Alaska, the sun does not rise at all between November 18 and January 22, so the community has about two months of solid night. A bit farther south, in Fairbanks, Alaska, residents do not experience a night that lasts for weeks. However, their nights in deepest winter are more than 20 hours long—leaving winter days of less than 4 hours.

Leopard seals rely on a layer of blubber (fat) to keep them warm. The layer of blubber is usually 1 to 6 inches (2.5 to 15 centimeters) thick.

Life in icy worlds

Animals, plants, and people living in icy places have **adapted** (adjusted or changed) over time to cold conditions. Their ways of life differ from those of living things inhabiting other world regions.

Some animals have adapted by growing heavy coats of fur to keep them warm in bitterly cold conditions. Some even change their coats from dark to white in winter to help them hide among the snow and ice.

Sea mammals have adapted to the cold by developing a layer of fat called blubber under their skin. They can dive in freezing seawater for food with no ill effects from the cold. Among such animals are seals and penguins.

People living in cold regions have become experts at surviving cold conditions. For example, many people of these regions hunt animals and sew warm coats out of the animals' skins. They also, on occasion, build structures made from blocks of packed snow.

The Polar Regions

Earth has two polar regions. They are the Arctic, surrounding the North Pole, and the Antarctic, surrounding the South Pole. Each pole receives less direct sunlight than other parts of the globe.

The Arctic and Antarctic circles

The North and South poles are the two ends of Earth's **axis.** Geographers also draw lines of latitude (lines going east to west) and longitude (lines going north to south) on a globe.

Geographers mark a special line of latitude near each pole. The Arctic Circle is a line of latitude that lies 1,624 miles (2,613 kilometers) south of the North Pole. The Antarctic Circle is a line of latitude the very same distance north of the South Pole. In each case, the circle marks the greatest distance from the pole at which the sun never rises on the shortest day of the year and never sets on the longest day.

The Arctic polar region

The Arctic region surrounds the North Pole. That spot lies in the middle of the Arctic Ocean. Because the Arctic Ocean is so far north, much of it is covered with ice for most or all of the year.

At the edges of the Arctic Ocean are islands and continents that are mainly frigid, icy places. The northern parts of North America, Europe, and Asia border the Arctic Ocean. So does Greenland, the world's largest island.

The Arctic (left) is an ocean surrounded by continents. Polar ice, shown in white, covers the Arctic at the North Pole. The Antarctic is an ice-covered continent (shown in pink) surrounded by the Southern Ocean. Sea ice (shown in white) extends beyond the continent.

An Inuit village sits alongside a massive **iceberg** in Greenland. Inuit are a people who live in and near the Arctic.

The Antarctic polar region

The Antarctic region is quite different from the Arctic. That is because a vast continent, Antarctica, lies at its center. The South Pole is on this continent.

Bodies of water and land masses absorb and hold heat in different ways. Water in seas, oceans, and lakes heats up more slowly than land. But it holds heat longer. Land masses change temperature more rapidly than water. They do not hold heat for very long. These differences help explain why the South Pole is colder than the North Pole. The South Pole lies on a continent, whereas the North Pole lies in an ocean.

Antarctica is a harsher place than the Arctic. This is one reason that people began to explore the region only about 100 years ago. Also, people do not live in Antarctica except in specially built scientific stations.

Words, Words, Words

The words *latitude* and *longitude* both come from Latin.

- *Latitude* is from the Latin *latitudo*, meaning "breadth" or "width."
- *Longitude* is from the Latin *longitudo*, meaning "long."

Ice and snow cover 98 percent of the Antarctic continent. High mountain peaks and a few other bare rocky areas make up the only visible land.

High, Icy Places

The polar regions make up the largest icy worlds on Earth. However, some high mountain peaks are often covered in ice.

Why are mountaintops cold?

Very high mountain regions are often cold and icy most of the year or even year-round. This is because the temperature of air drops as you rise above the surface of Earth. The temperature drops about 3 or 4 Fahrenheit degrees (2 or 3 Celsius degrees) for each 1,000-foot (300-meter) increase in altitude.

Ice surrounded by desert

Surprising as it may seem, Africa's highest mountain, Kilimanjaro, usually has snow and ice on its highest peak year-round. Kilimanjaro is only about 200 miles (322 kilometers) from the equator. However, its highest peak is 19,340 feet (5,895 meters) high. Even in the hottest part of Earth, that altitude causes bitterly cold temperatures.

Icy places on mountaintops are different from those in the polar regions. They are small pockets of cold regions surrounded by warmer lands. A warming trend in Earth's **climate** could change such icy pockets on mountains more quickly than most other parts of the planet.

Mount Everest is the highest mountain in the world. It is part of the Himalaya range on the frontier of Tibet and Nepal. The lofty, snow-covered peak rises about 5 ½ miles (8.9 kilometers) above sea level.

A giraffe walks across Kenya's dry, hot grasslands below towering Mount Kilimanjaro. Although the mountain is in equatorial Africa, one of Kilimanjaro's three peaks, Kibo, is usually covered by snow and ice.

Masses of ice

Some of the world's greatest mountain chains have many high peaks with large areas of ice and snow. (A mountain chain is a long row of connected mountains.) High, icy places occur in many of these mountain chains.

The icy world of high mountain peaks features snow and ice packs that have built up over time. On occasion, the weight of snow and ice on a mountain slope causes it to be unsteady. A disturbance, such as a strong wind, may send the snow and ice tumbling down the mountain in an avalanche. Avalanches sometimes bury houses or even entire villages under tons of snow and ice.

So much snow accumulates on some high mountains that its weight presses down, crushing the snow into a mass of ice. The packed snow has become an icy **glacier.** Gravity causes glaciers to flow slowly from higher to lower places.

Top of the World

For many years, adventurous explorers tried and failed to reach the top of Mount Everest. Finally, in May 1953, Sir Edmund Hillary and his guide, Tenzing Norgay, reached Everest's highest peak at "the top of the world." Mount Everest, the world's highest mountain, is in the Himalaya, between the nations of Nepal and Tibet. It soars 29,035 feet (8,850 meters) above sea level.

The call of Everest is still strong. Even today, small groups of experienced climbers accept the mountain's challenge. But the dangers are great. Ferocious snowstorms can blow up almost without warning. Temperatures may suddenly drop to dangerous levels at which exposed skin freezes in mere seconds.

▼ Mountains of the World

Arctic Ocean

Rocky Mountains

NORTH AMERICA

EUROPE

Ural Mountains

Alps

Caucasus Mountains

ASIA

Atlas Mts.

Himalaya

Mount Everest

Pacific Ocean

AFRICA

Atlantic Ocean

Equator

Kilimanjaro

Indian Ocean

Equator

Pacific Ocean

SOUTH AMERICA

Andes Mountains

AUSTRALIA

ANTARCTICA

Ice That Comes and Goes

Some lands are icy and cold in winter but warm and ice-free in the summer. These lands are called the temperate regions. Temperate regions lie between the hot equatorial regions and the cold polar regions.

Earth's seasons

The tilt in Earth's **axis** is responsible for the seasons. As Earth moves around the sun, it stays nearly the same distance from the sun throughout the year. However, the tilt of Earth's axis changes the amount of sunlight a **temperate region** receives throughout the year. The area is in summer when it receives much sunlight. The area is in winter when it receives little sunlight. Spring and fall are the "in-between" seasons.

Differences between seasons in temperate regions can be extreme. In North Dakota, winter temperatures have sunk as low as –60 °F (–51 °C). But in summer, temperatures have soared to 121 °F (49 °C). In many other temperate regions, seasonal differences are significant but not as extreme.

In many temperate regions, the peak of fall is marked by the changing color of the leaves.

Snowstorms are a common feature of winter in many parts of the world.

Rain, snow, sleet, hail

Lands in temperate regions receive a variety of **precipitation.** Rain falls for much of the year. Sometimes in winter, such frozen forms of precipitation as snow and sleet (tiny ice pellets) fall. Occasionally in summer, frozen precipitation called hail falls from big thunderstorms. Hail ranges from little ice pellets to lumps of ice the size of grapefruits.

Frozen precipitation may pile up on the ground. But in time, warmer temperatures eventually melt it. Snow and ice do not accumulate year after year in temperate lands.

Life in temperate regions

Animals and plants in temperate regions have **adapted** over time to their seasonal conditions. For example, many types of trees shed their leaves in fall. Then they grow new leaves in spring. Trees that are not adapted to cold seasons—such as palms—cannot survive cold winters in temperate regions.

People living in temperate regions make changes to live with seasonal conditions. They wear heavy, warm clothes in winter. In summer, they may wear shorts and tank tops. Also, people in temperate regions close their homes up tightly in winter and heat them. But in warmer seasons, they open their windows and let in fresh, outside air.

A thunderstorm moves over the city of Dresden, Germany.

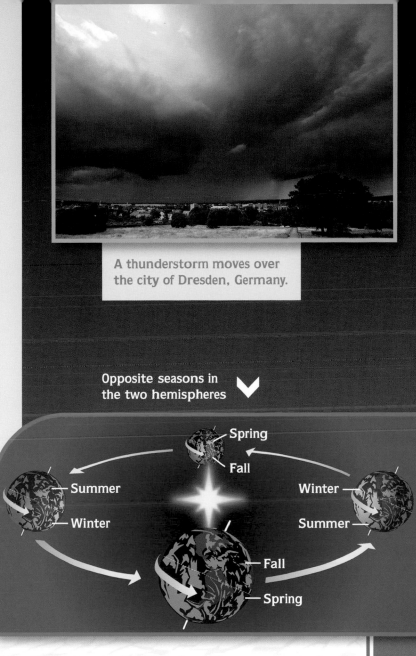

Opposite seasons in the two hemispheres

Summer or Winter?

The Northern and Southern hemispheres both have seasons—but they are the opposite of each other. The tilt in Earth's axis creates the seasons. When the tilt of the axis brings more sunlight to the Northern Hemisphere, the Southern Hemisphere gets less sunlight. It is then summer in the North and winter in the South. Half a year later, the opposite is true.

Ice Ages

Earth's climate changes slowly over time. At times in the past, Earth has been warmer than it is today. At other times, it has been colder. Very cold periods in Earth's long history are called ice ages.

In an ice age, all of Earth cools down. As a result, more frozen **precipitation** falls over a wider area. Snow piles up, creating **glaciers.** In time, the glaciers merge into immense **ice sheets.** The ice sheets begin to flatten and spread out from their starting point toward open land because of their sheer weight.

Between ice ages

Long periods between ice ages are called interglacial periods. All of Earth warms up. Ice melts and ice sheets shrink or disappear entirely.

We are in an interglacial period now. There is far less ice on Earth today than there was about 11,500 years ago, when the most recent ice age ended.

Why does Earth warm up and cool down from time to time? Most scientists think that small changes in Earth's orbit (path around the sun) and the tilt of its **axis** cause these changes. Earth's orbit slowly changes the planet's distance from the sun. This affects the strength of the sunlight it receives. Stronger sunlight leads to warmer temperatures. Weaker sunlight leads to colder temperatures.

Did You Know?

During the last ice age, sea levels fell so far that a land bridge appeared between northeastern Asia and the part of North America we know as Alaska. Some bands of hunters from Asia crossed into North America using this land bridge, possibly following such big game as woolly mammoths. In time, many thousands of these hunters crossed into North America. (Other groups, which came earlier, would have used a different route.) These groups are ancestors of the people we now know as Native Americans.

In the most recent ice age, which ended about 11,500 years ago, ice sheets covered vast areas in the Northern Hemisphere. During their farthest advance, shown on this map, the ice sheets covered what are now the Scandinavian countries and other northern parts of Europe, and most of Canada. Ice sheets also covered Antarctica, but they were less extensive in the Southern Hemisphere.

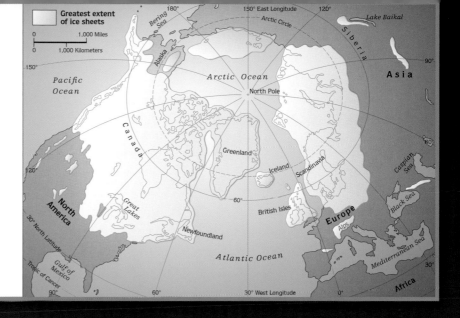

The Ice Ages

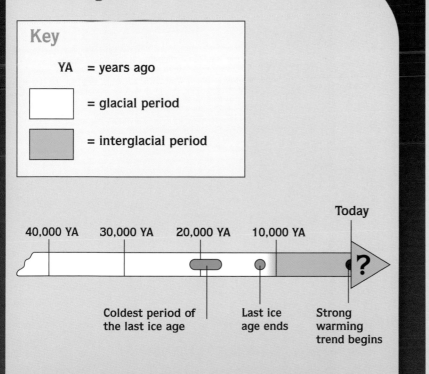

Key

YA = years ago

☐ = glacial period

▨ = interglacial period

40,000 YA   30,000 YA   20,000 YA   10,000 YA   Today

Coldest period of the last ice age

Last ice age ends

Strong warming trend begins

Rising and falling seas

Earth has a steady supply of water. Water can exist in the form of liquid, gas, or solid ice. Liquid water is constantly undergoing evaporation from oceans, lakes, and rivers. In evaporation, liquid water changes to water vapor, a gas. This water vapor in the air forms clouds and causes precipitation over land.

During an ice age, much of the precipitation is in a frozen form, such as snow or sleet. Over time, it piles up to great heights on land—rather than running off, as rain would do. As more water is locked up on land as ice, the world's sea level drops.

During the last ice age, sea level was at least 330 feet (100 meters) lower than it is today. Many areas that are today under water along coasts were once dry land.

Glaciers

Glaciers are huge masses of solid ice that move slowly over the land. Glaciers form in the colder regions near the North and South poles and in mountainous areas.

How glaciers form

Glaciers form in areas where some snow remains on the ground throughout the year. This snow can accumulate (pile up) in layers over hundreds or even thousands of years. Eventually, the weight of the upper snow layers compresses the lower layers into tiny pellets of ice called firn. At greater depths, the weight further compresses firn into solid ice. As snow turns into firn and ice, the frozen mass becomes more dense. With enough pressure, the ice can begin to flow, and the mass becomes a glacier.

Meltwater (water from melted ice) plays an important role in the formation of most glaciers. As ice on the glacier's surface melts, meltwater seeps deep into the ice mass, filling open spaces between ice crystals and particles and then refreezing.

Mountain glaciers

A common place for glaciers to form is in high mountain valleys or cirques (bowl-like hollows). High mountains are cold places because temperature decreases (falls) as the altitude gets higher. Also, high mountains tend to lift air masses, causing much **precipitation** to fall. Very high mountain regions, such as high peaks in the Andes Mountains (in western South America) and the Himalaya (in Asia), are always cold and often snowy. Glaciers fill many high valleys in the Andes, the Himalaya, and other high mountain chains.

The Mendenhall Glacier is a popular tourist attraction near Juneau, Alaska. The glacier extends 12 miles (19.3 kilometers) from the Juneau Icefield to Mendenhall Lake.

Taku Glacier cuts through the Coast Mountains in Alaska.

How glaciers move

Mountain glaciers move because of the pull of gravity. As a glacier builds, its weight tends to push it from higher to lower ground. Most mountain and valley glaciers move very slowly. However, as the glacier reaches lower altitude and, thus, warmer temperatures, it begins to speed up. Meltwater from the glacier runs around and under the ice. It lubricates the glacier (makes it slippery). Some glaciers slide all the way to an arm of the sea or to the sea itself. Big chunks of ice then calve (break off) from the edge of the glacier and float away. These ice chunks are called **icebergs.**

Features of glaciers

Valley glaciers can be hundreds of feet or meters deep. They can be tens of miles or kilometers long. The top of a glacier may look smooth from a distance. However, its surface is broken up by many narrow, deep cracks. One such crack is called a crevasse. Some crevasses are hundreds of feet (meters) deep. They create very dangerous conditions for people who explore glaciers.

In warmer seasons, small pools of meltwater sometimes appear on the surface of a glacier. Often, the water disappears quickly as it runs down a crevasse.

▲ A climber descends into a crevasse on an ice cliff in Antarctica.

Ice Sheets

Some glaciers form when snow piles up year after year over a very wide expanse of land. In time, a thick blanket of glacial ice covers the land. Such glaciers are called continental glaciers, or ice sheets.

The Greenland ice sheet covers nearly all land on the island.

Polar ice sheets

The continent of Antarctica is covered by an **ice sheet.** On average, the Antarctic ice sheet is about 11,500 feet (3,500 meters) thick. Steep walls of ice from this **glacier** meet the sea at the edges of Antarctica.

Another ice sheet covers most of Greenland, the world's largest island. Greenland lies off the northeastern coast of North America. It is part of the Arctic region. The Greenland ice sheet averages more than 1 mile (1.6 kilometers) thick, and a thickness of over 2 miles (3.2 kilometers) has been measured.

Massive and heavy

A continental glacier presses down on the solid ground beneath with tremendous weight and pressure. This pressure causes the ice sheet to push out at the edges. In time, the ice sheet can cover an entire continent, as in Antarctica. As the ice sheet pushes outward into a sea or ocean, it forms **icebergs.**

The weight of an ice sheet is such that it even depresses the solid ground underneath it. In Greenland, scientists estimate that the continental ice sheet has depressed some underlying ground as much as 1,000 feet (300 meters) below sea level. If the Greenland ice sheet melted, this land would gradually rise as the weight above it decreased.

A research vessel navigates around Antarctic ice sheets.

Telltale Signs

When glaciers melt and shrink, they leave many telltale signs on the land. **Geologists** can read these signs to estimate the size, shape, and position of a long-gone glacier. Here are some features that a geologist looks for.

- Moraine: a long, low ridge of soil and rock deposited along the sides or edge of a glacier
- Drumlin: a small, oval-shaped hill
- Esker: a narrow, winding ridge caused by sand running through a tunnel in ice
- Kettle: a small, round pond caused when a chunk of buried ice melts
- Striations: long grooves scratched into rock by glacial ice

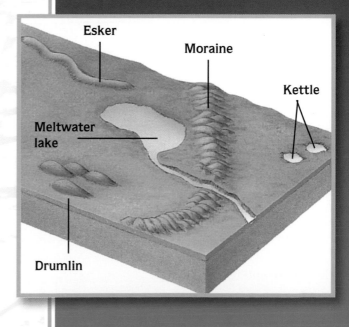

Esker

Moraine

Kettle

Meltwater lake

Drumlin

Sea Ice

Ice forms on the surface of the ocean in places where air temperatures stay very cold for a long period. This ice is called sea ice.

The sea ice surrounding Antarctica is broken up by ocean swells in late summer.

If you live in a **temperate region,** you probably know that it takes little time for a small puddle of water to turn into ice on a cold winter night. But you may wonder why the ocean never becomes covered with ice in areas with cold winters.

To begin with, the water in oceans is salty. Salt, along with other **minerals** dissolved in seawater, lowers the freezing temperature several degrees. In addition, the constant movement of the ocean helps prevent it from freezing over. Large bodies of water also absorb and release heat much more slowly than land. For these reasons, seawater freezes only when in contact with bitterly cold air for a long period. Sea ice forms only in polar regions.

Sea ice floats

Which is heavier—frozen or liquid water? It might seem that hard, rigid ice would be heavier. However, liquid water is heavier than frozen water. That is why ice cubes float in a glass of water. In the same way, sea ice floats on the surface of seas and oceans.

Sea ice covers much of the Arctic Ocean's surface. Chunks of glacial ice form **icebergs,** seen in the distance in this photo.

Arctic sea ice

The Arctic Ocean surrounds the North Pole. Bitterly cold Arctic air keeps more than half of the area of this ocean frozen year-round. Most of the rest of the ocean freezes in winter but thaws in summer. The permanently frozen sea ice can be up to 15 feet (5 meters) thick in some places. Edges of this polar ice mass are thinner and more subject to melting. Watery channels called leads separate some of these edge sections.

Antarctic sea ice

The South Pole is covered by a land mass rather than an ocean. However, the oceans around the edges of the continent of Antarctica freeze outward about 1,000 miles (1,600 kilometers) from the coast in winter. In summer, the ice breaks up into pieces called **ice floes.** Winds and waves then push the floes against one another, forming thick ice masses called pack ice. Pack ice sometimes piles up in icy ridges against the Antarctic shore.

A Canadian Coast Guard icebreaker and Arctic research vessel trolls through the Amundsen Gulf in spring.

Icebergs

Huge chunks of ice can break off the lower end of a glacier and fall into the sea. These masses are called icebergs, and they are made of frozen fresh water. Fog and icebergs are two of the greatest natural dangers to ships.

An iceberg floats in the Atlantic Ocean near Newfoundland, Canada.

Masses of floating ice

Icebergs can be enormous. Many weigh more than 1 million tons (910,000 metric tons). Some tower 400 feet (120 meters) above the ocean's surface.

Most icebergs are white because of the tightly packed snow of which they are made. However, some icebergs are blue. In these icebergs, the snow and ice have been packed so densely that the light scatters, rather like light in a blue sky. And some icebergs are green. Such icebergs contain vast numbers of tiny plantlike organisms called **algae.**

Icebergs in the Northern Hemisphere

Most icebergs in the Northern Hemisphere break off from **glaciers** in Greenland and float in the North Atlantic Ocean. The largest iceberg ever observed in the North Atlantic was about 4 miles (6.4 kilometers) long.

An Iceberg for Your Tea?

In the 1970's, a Saudi Arabian prince sponsored a scientific conference on icebergs. The prince asked scientists to consider the possibility of towing icebergs from Antarctic waters to such desert countries as Saudi Arabia. Icebergs consist of fresh water, so they could be melted down to provide drinking water. Over the years, people have continued to discuss this idea—but it has never actually been tried on a large scale.

It was said to be "unsinkable." The *Titanic*, one of the largest, most luxurious passenger ships ever built, set out from Southampton, England, on April 10, 1912. The ship's steady course westward toward New York City was uneventful—until the night of April 14. Running almost at top speed, the *Titanic* struck an iceberg in the North Atlantic Ocean about 400 miles (650 kilometers) southeast of Newfoundland. Within two and a half hours, the ship had broken in two and sunk. About 1,500 people lost their lives in the disaster. The tragedy of the *Titanic* revealed the dangers of icebergs to shipping as nothing before or since.

Icebergs in the Southern Hemisphere

Most icebergs in the Southern Hemisphere break off from glaciers along the coast of Antarctica. Antarctic icebergs drift into the Southern Ocean, which surrounds Antarctica.

Some Antarctic icebergs are many times larger than the largest Arctic icebergs. The largest iceberg ever observed in Antarctic waters was about 200 miles (320 kilometers) long and about 60 miles (97 kilometers) wide—about the size of the U.S. state of Connecticut.

Navigational hazards

Icebergs pose great danger to ships. The part of an iceberg that is underwater is often much larger than the visible part above the waterline. If a ship smashes into an iceberg, it is likely to be seriously damaged and even sink. Shipping nations and the U.S. Coast Guard patrol shipping lanes in the North Atlantic Ocean for icebergs and issue warnings to ships when necessary.

Lands and Seas of the Arctic

The region of continuous cold around the North Pole is known as the Arctic. The Arctic region includes the Arctic Ocean, Greenland and many other islands, and northern fringes of Asia, Europe, and North America.

Waters of the Arctic

The North Pole lies in the Arctic Ocean, far from any land. Seawater in the polar icecap surrounding the North Pole is always frozen. Areas of the Arctic Ocean farther away from the pole have a solid ice pack in winter. But in summer, the ice pack breaks up into free-floating **ice floes.**

Types of land

Lands of the Arctic are not all alike. Greenland is almost entirely covered by a thick **ice sheet.** This ice sheet covers the ground year-round. However, most Arctic lands are free of ice in the summer.

Most lands of the Arctic are too cold to support trees. These treeless areas are called **tundra.** Only small plants can grow on tundra. These include grasses, mosses, and **lichens.** Mosses are small plants that grow as thick mats. They lack flowers or true roots. Lichens look like plants but are actually fungi, like mushrooms. These fungi live with **algae,** which grow as pond scum in warmer areas. Lichens are so tough they can grow on bare rock.

Another important feature of Arctic lands is **permafrost.** Permafrost is ground that is frozen most or all of the time. In summer, the uppermost layers of permafrost melt. As a result, many Arctic lands in summer are filled with swampy **bogs** called muskegs where mosquitoes and other insects breed.

Wildflowers bloom across the tundra landscape in Skaftafell National Park in Iceland.

The Arctic tern migrates all the way from the Arctic to Antarctica each year.

Arctic deep freeze

You might expect the coldest spot in the Arctic to be the North Pole itself. However, the coldest temperature ever recorded in the Arctic was in Siberia. In this region, the temperature dropped to –44 °F (–68 °C) on February 7, 1892, and again on February 6, 1933. Land easily loses its heat in the dark cold of winter. Water stays warmer. This difference explains why the coldest Arctic temperature occurred on land more than 1,000 miles (1,600 kilometers) from the North Pole.

Countries of the Arctic

A handful of countries control most of the lands of the Arctic. A large swath of the North American Arctic is Canadian land. The Canadian Arctic stretches from Newfoundland and Labrador in the east to the Yukon Territory in the West. It includes many islands.

Just east of Canada is Greenland, a semi-independent country with ties to Denmark. Northern parts of Alaska, a U.S. state, are Arctic lands to the west of Canada.

Russia controls more than 4,000 miles (6,300 kilometers) of Arctic lands stretching along its northern coast. Siberia, the vast eastern part of Russia, makes up much of this Arctic territory. Northern parts of Finland, Norway, and Sweden are in the Arctic.

What's in a Name?

The name *Arctic* comes from *arktikos*, a Greek word meaning "North Star." The North Star is a very bright star seen in the far northern night sky in the Northern Hemisphere.

The name *Antarctica* was formed by adding the Greek prefix *Ant-* to *Arktikos*. The prefix means "the opposite of," so *Antarktikos*, or *Antarctica*, means "the opposite of the *Arctic*."

Map of the Arctic

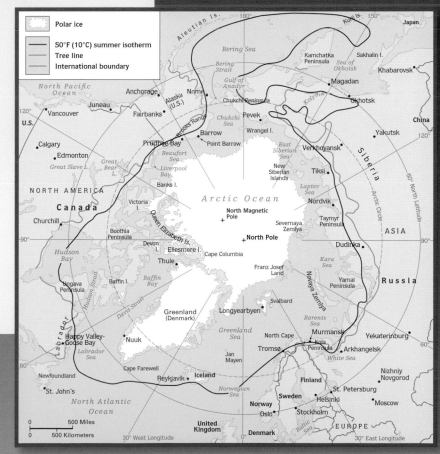

Arctic Explorers

The first Europeans to explore the Arctic after the Vikings were English sea captains of the 1500's. People first visited the North Pole itself in the early 1900's.

Early exploration

Native Americans settled in Arctic regions thousands of years ago. However, people living in most other parts of the world knew little or nothing about Arctic lands for a very long time.

Around 1,000 years ago, Vikings, a seafaring people from Scandinavia, began to settle in Iceland and Greenland. Then in the late 1500's and early 1600's, a few European explorers visited Arctic regions in northeastern Canada. They were seeking the Northwest Passage, a sea passage through North America to the Pacific Ocean. Among these sea captains were Martin Frobisher, John Davis, and Henry Hudson of England.

The biggest challenge

More serious exploration of Arctic regions began in the 1800's. In the late 1800's, explorers from a number of countries began to compete for the honor of being the first to reach the North Pole. Traveling to the North Pole would prove to be almost unimaginably difficult. It exposed explorers to fierce storms and dangerously cold temperatures. But perhaps the biggest challenge was traveling over many hundreds of miles of sea ice. The only way to cover the distance over sea ice was with dogsleds pulled by Siberian huskies. The sleds carried food and all the other supplies needed by the explorers.

Robert Peary stands aboard the deck of his ship, *Roosevelt*, in 1909.

Sounds at the Top of the World

Explorers camping on the polar ice pack surrounding the North Pole hear loud, frightening sounds they describe as squeals, screams, rumbling, and groaning. Movement in the seas beneath the ice cause the ice to buckle, crack, slip, and slide. Every change in the ice pack gives off strange noises.

To the pole

In 1908 and early 1909, U.S. Navy Captain Robert E. Peary led a successful **expedition** (journey) from Ellesmere Island, in the Canadian Arctic, to the North Pole. According to Peary's records, he reached the North Pole on April 6, 1909. But when Peary returned to the United States, another American explorer—Frederick A. Cook—claimed to have reached the pole in 1908. Many historians credit Peary's claim, but no one knows for certain who reached the pole first.

U.S. Navy Admiral Richard Byrd claimed to have been the first person to fly an airplane over the North Pole, in 1926. Today, some historians doubt Byrd's claim. In 1958, the U.S. nuclear-powered submarine *Nautilus* passed underneath Arctic ice and crossed the North Pole.

In recent times

People today are still taking up the challenge of North Pole exploration. In 1994, a Norwegian explorer named Borge Ousland went by foot alone over the sea ice to the North Pole. In 2006, Ousland and South African explorer Mike Horn became the first to travel unassisted to the North Pole in the complete darkness of winter.

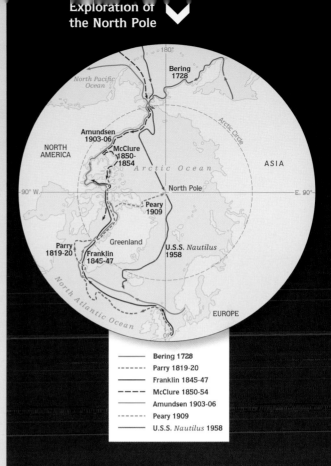

Exploration of the North Pole

———	Bering 1728
- - - -	Parry 1819-20
———	Franklin 1845-47
– – –	McClure 1850-54
———	Amundsen 1903-06
- - - -	Peary 1909
———	U.S.S. *Nautilus* 1958

Did You Know?

Sled-dog teams that are properly trained can travel at average speeds of 20 miles (30 kilometers) per hour.

Plant Life of the Arctic

Most plants that grow in the Arctic are small and hardy. Many grow in swampy areas during the Arctic summer.

Most Arctic lands are treeless **tundra**. However, lush plant life grows even in these harsh lands. Although true Arctic lands are too cold to support trees and most shrubs, they host thick carpets of smaller plants that burst forth with vibrant color in the brief Arctic summer.

Arctic bogs

Swampy Arctic plains support vast **bogs** in which mosses flourish. A bog consists chiefly of decayed or decaying moss and other plant matter. The spongy surface of a bog is too soft to bear the weight of any heavy body.

One of the more common mosses is called sphagnum *(SFAG nuhm)* moss, also known as peat moss. The leaves of sphagnum moss are tiny, but together the plants form a strong, dense mat of vegetation. These carpets of moss may be deep brown, red, or yellow-green in color. Over time, layers of sphagnum moss pack down and sink, forming a decayed substance called peat.

Lands of the Arctic also support many kinds of **lichens** *(LY kuhns)*. Lichens provide food for many Arctic animals.

Despite the short growing season, plant life abounds on the Arctic tundra during summer.

Arctic cotton grass grows in cold bogs and swampy land. >

Cushion plant

The cushion plant (also called moss campion) is another plant that grows in the Arctic. Although cushion plants form a dense mat like mosses, they are actually flowering plants. Cushion plants are well **adapted** for survival in a cold **climate.** They grow slowly and flower only in favorable years. The flowers are tiny.

Other Arctic plants

Arctic lands also grow a variety of grasses and sedges (reedlike plants). These plants are well suited to cold, swampy conditions.

Some flowers grow in the Arctic as well. In July, during the Arctic summer, the tundra in many places comes alive with colorful blooms.

One common wildflower of the Arctic is purple saxifrage (*SAK suh frihj*). Saxifrage has flat, fleshy leaves that grow near the ground. The round, purple flowers grow on stalks above the leaves. Saxifrage tolerates cold and can grow even in dry cracks between rocks.

Other wildflowers bloom during the Arctic summer. Among them are cinquefoil (*SIHNGK foyl*), Arctic poppy, and Arctic lupine.

Adaptations of Arctic Plants

To survive, plants of the Arctic have adapted to the harsh conditions.

- Arctic plants go dormant when it turns cold—that is, they slow down all life processes and become less sensitive to bitter cold.

- Arctic plants need little water to survive. For example, some Arctic plants have thick, fleshy leaves that store water.

- Arctic plants grow rapidly during the brief summer.

- Flowering plants make seeds only when conditions are exactly right. The seeds are so tough that they can survive the bitterest cold.

Saxifrage is a group of hardy plants that grow in the Arctic. These plants usually grow on or between rocks. In fact, the word *saxifrage* means rock-breaker.

Animal Life of the Arctic

The Arctic region is home to a wide variety of animal life. Animals live both on lands and in seas of the Arctic.

Land animals

Many animals live on the Arctic **tundra.** Among them are caribou, ermine (a member of the weasel family), musk oxen, reindeer, lemmings, snowy owls, and wolves. Mosquitoes and other insects lay their eggs in pools of water in **bogs.** These insects provide food for birds that migrate (travel) to the tundra each summer to nest.

In some parts of the Arctic, vast herds of caribou graze on lush plains in summer. In winter, they dig through snow to find **lichens** to eat. One such place is the Arctic National Wildlife Refuge (ANWR) in northern Alaska.

Snowy owls breed on the Arctic tundra.

Caribou are large deer of the Arctic. Their broad hoofs keep them from sinking into snow or bogs. This male has scraped the fleshy velvet from the antlers he will use to fight other males.

A bowhead whale breaches in the waters surrounding Nunavut, Canada.

Ocean animals

Seas of the Arctic are home to abundant animal life. Many kinds of fish, giant sponges, and small shrimplike animals called **krill** live in the ocean waters. Other land-dwelling animals spend much of their time on floating sheets of ice on Arctic waters. Among these animals are polar bears, seals, sea lions, and walruses. Polar bears hunt seals and small whales. Seals, sea lions, and walruses hunt mainly fish, krill, and squid.

Many whales come to Arctic waters in the summer. Beluga whales swim in open waters during the summer. They migrate southward in winter, when these waters freeze over.

A group of male narwhals gather to feed at the edge of the ice. Narwhals are Arctic whales known for their long, spiral tusks.

People of the Arctic

Over thousands of years, many different groups of people have settled in the Arctic region. They come from a variety of backgrounds, but all have learned to live under the harsh conditions.

Changes to native culture

Traditionally, Arctic people have all made clothing from animal skins. The people have hunted on land and at sea for meat and fish or have herded reindeer.

Today, many people of the Arctic have adopted a modern lifestyle. For example, they often wear factory-made clothes. Many people live in modern houses and use vehicles and boats for transportation. Many also work at jobs where they earn wages used to buy food and other necessities.

The Inuit

One group of people in the Arctic—the Inuit—inhabit Arctic lands from Greenland all the way to the Siberian coast of the Bering Sea. The Inuit language is similar throughout the Arctic. Today, many Inuit earn wages and do not depend solely on hunting and fishing for a living. Inuit are often called Eskimos in Alaska, but the Inuit in Greenland and Alaska do not like the term.

A Yakut herder stands with his reindeer near the town of Verkhoyansk in Siberia.

Inuit children gather during a school break on Baffin Island, off the northern coast of Canada.

Peoples of the Siberian Arctic

The Siberian Arctic stretches for more than 4,000 miles (6,300 kilometers) along the northern coast of Russia. Many different ethnic groups populate this vast area. The most numerous group is the Yakuts. Many of the Yakuts hunt, fish, and herd reindeer for a living. Others live more modern ways of life.

In the far northeastern corner of Siberia, directly opposite Alaska, live the Koryak, Itclman, and Chukchi tribes. The people of these tribes fish and hunt. Some herd reindeer.

Peoples of the European Arctic

Traditional peoples of the Arctic also inhabit the far northern regions of Scandinavia and European Russia. Most of these groups are related to the people of Finland. They speak languages related to Finnish.

Sami are the native peoples of northern Norway, Sweden, Finland, and the far north-western corner of Russia. Traditionally, they are reindeer herders. Today, many Sami work in fishing, lumbering, or other occupations as wage earners.

Words, Words, Words

Some Inuit words have made their way into English. Several are listed below.

English Word	Definition
anorak	a waterproof jacket
igloo	a house made of ice blocks
kayak	a canoe
malamute	a breed of dog
mukluk	a fur-lined boot
parka[1]	a hooded jacket

[1] *from Aleut, a language of the Arctic that is related to Inuit*

A Sami mother and daughter wear traditional dress. ⌄

Arctic Warming

The Arctic region has been very cold and icy for more than a million years. But in recent years, the Arctic has been warming. In fact, all of Earth is experiencing a warming trend called global warming. The rate of warming is not the same in all places.

Heating up

Scientists have strong evidence that Earth's average surface temperature rose by about 1.4 degrees Fahrenheit (0.76 degrees Celsius) from the mid-1800's to the early 2000's. The warming has been especially rapid since the mid-1900's.

Climate scientists believe that the burning of fossil fuels (coal, oil, and natural gas) and other human activities are the main cause of the recent warming. Fossil fuels are burned for many purposes. We use gasoline and similar fuels to run cars, trucks, trains, and jets. We use coal in many power plants to produce electricity. People use natural gas to heat their homes. Many scientists warn that **global warming** will speed up unless people cut back sharply on their use of fossil fuels.

An icebreaker moves through sea ice during the Arctic summer. Sea ice currently blankets waters around the northern coast of North America. However, some scientists predict that global warming may create a passage through these waters as sea ice continues to melt.

The amount of carbon dioxide in Earth's atmosphere has increased since the beginning of the Industrial Revolution in about 1750 and more rapidly since about 1950.

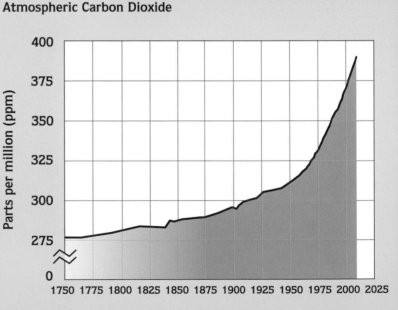

Atmospheric Carbon Dioxide

y-axis: Parts per million (ppm) — 400, 375, 350, 325, 300, 275, 0

x-axis: 1750 1775 1800 1825 1850 1875 1900 1925 1950 1975 2000 2025

Source: World Book estimates based on Antarctic ice core data; National Oceanic and Atmospheric Administration.

The greenhouse effect

When people burn fossil fuels, carbon dioxide and other gases are released into the **atmosphere.** Carbon dioxide (CO_2) is a colorless, odorless gas. We breathe out CO_2, and a small part of Earth's atmosphere is made up of the gas. However, the amount of CO_2 in the atmosphere has increased by about 40 percent since 1750.

In Earth's atmosphere, CO_2 and other gases act like the glass walls of a greenhouse, trapping heat. For this reason, it is referred to as a **greenhouse gas.** The more CO_2 there is in the atmosphere, the warmer Earth gets.

Uneven heating

As Earth's average temperature warms over time, heating is not even. Some places are warming faster than others. Polar regions are warming faster than other parts of the planet. In fact, the Arctic has warmed about twice as fast as the rest of Earth. Climate scientists believe that this trend will get even worse in the future. Global warming could greatly change the Arctic in our lifetimes.

Solar radiation

Some radiation is reflected off the surface and the atmosphere.

Some radiation is trapped by greenhouse gases, warming the planet.

The greenhouse effect traps heat from the sun. This complex process involves sunlight, gases, and atmospheric particles.

Then and Now

Earth's climate has changed over time. About 3 million years ago, Greenland was so warm it had no **ice sheet.** But climate is changing more quickly than normal today. The loss of Greenland's ice sheet would raise sea levels and flood coastal areas. Most living things would survive, but millions of people would suffer.

Rapid climate change in the Arctic

Temperatures in the Arctic have risen about twice as fast as the global average. One sign of this change is the loss of sea ice in the Arctic Ocean.

Almost all of the Arctic Ocean is covered by sea ice in winter. During summer, part of the sea ice melts, leaving some open ocean water.

In September 2007, the Arctic sea ice shrank to the smallest area ever recorded. The area covered by the sea ice was over 30 percent less than the average during the late 1900's. Summer sea ice has remained low since 2007.

Sea ice helps keep the Arctic cold. The white ice reflects sunlight back into space. Open ocean water is dark. It absorbs sunlight and warms the ocean. The less summer sea ice there is, the more the remaining ice will melt. Disappearing sea ice will make the Arctic warm even more quickly.

The Arctic climate has warmed significantly in the past few decades, causing a reduction in sea ice in the Arctic Ocean.

A small island in the Bay of Bengal became submerged due to rising sea levels in 2009-2010. Scientists attributed the disappearance of the island to the combined forces of erosion and rising sea levels. Other low-lying coastal islands may face a similar fate as global warming melts polar ice and Earth's seas rise.

Winners and losers

Global warming will make life in the Arctic easier for people in some ways. Farmers in Canada and Siberia could raise crops farther north. But global warming also melts **permafrost.** That can cause buildings to collapse.

Global warming could harm many Arctic animals. Polar bears hunt seals from **ice floes.** If sea ice disappeared in the summer, many polar bears would starve. Many seals also would not survive. The sea ice also supports a huge number of tiny ocean animals. These provide food for larger animals. If the sea ice disappeared in the summer, countless crabs, fish, whales, and other animals would be harmed.

On land, global warming could cause trees to spread farther north, shrinking the **tundra.** That could harm many animals, including the Arctic fox, caribou, lemmings, and snowy owls. It would also impact the many birds that travel to the Arctic in the summer to breed. Other animals would be helped by a warmer Arctic. For example, many animals would live in the new forests.

The rest of the world

A warming Arctic is alarming news for many of the world's people. Sea level is rising by about ⅒ inch (3 millimeters) a year. About a quarter of that increase is from melting ice in Greenland. Scientists warn that sea levels could rise by more than 6 feet (2 meters) in the next 100 years. That would flood coastal areas and cause millions of people to suffer. It would take longer for the entire Greenland **ice sheet** to melt. But it could raise sea levels by more than 21 feet (7 meters).

▲ In Alaska, melting permafrost has caused some houses and other buildings to collapse.

Threatened Polar Bears

The number of polar bears is shrinking partly because of melting sea ice. Scientists reported that between 1987 and 2004, the polar bear population in western Hudson Bay, Canada, fell by 22 percent. Scientists estimate that there are between 20,000 and 25,000 polar bears in the world. The U.S. Department of the Interior has listed the polar bear as a threatened **species**. Many scientists fear that global warming could cause polar bears to become extinct.

Land and Seas of Antarctica

Almost all land in the Antarctic region is in a single land mass—the continent of Antarctica. The Antarctic region also includes the seas that surround that continent.

A thick blanket of ice

More land is covered by ice in Antarctica than in any other area of the world. This **ice sheet** is also deep. On average, Antarctica's blanket of ice is about 7,000 feet (2,200 meters) thick. However, in some places the ice sheet is as thick as 11,500 feet (3,500 meters).

Seas and coastal areas

The ocean waters that surround Antarctica are referred to as the Southern Ocean. However, there are no physical boundaries between these waters and the southern reaches of three other oceans: the Indian Ocean, the South Atlantic Ocean, and the South Pacific Ocean.

Permanent ice fills in many bays and inlets on the coastline of Antarctica. Also, **glaciers** slide into the ocean at some places on the Antarctic coast. Chunks of ice breaking off where ice slides into the ocean form **icebergs.** The icebergs float out into the Southern Ocean.

In winter, sea ice forms all around the edges of Antarctica. Typically, the ocean surface freezes outward as much as 1,000 miles (1,600 kilometers) from the coast by late winter. In summer, most of this ice breaks up.

Antarctica's rugged coast features jagged mountain peaks and glacier-filled valleys.

Did You Know?

The northernmost tip of the Antarctic Peninsula is about 650 miles (1,046 kilometers) from the southernmost tip of South America. That is about the same distance as between Winnipeg, Canada, and Milwaukee, Wisconsin, in the United States.

A hiker observes the view from Ice Tower Ridge on Mount Erebus in Antarctica. Steam and gases released from deep inside Earth helped to form such ice formations along a slope of the active volcano.

Mountains

The Transantarctic Mountains cross the entire Antarctic continent from the Weddell Sea to Ross Sea. This range includes mountains that are nearly 15,000 feet (4,570 meters) high. A few high mountains in this region have small dry valleys where snow has blown away. Antarctica's highest mountain is near the Antarctic Peninsula in West Antarctica. Called the Vinson Massif, it is 16,067 feet (4,897 meters) high. On Ross Island, off the coast of West Antarctica, stands Mount Erebus, Antarctica's most active volcano.

Natural divisions

Nearly all of Antarctica is covered with two massive ice sheets. The Transantarctic mountain range divides these two sections. East Antarctica is the huge area on the east side of the mountains. The South Pole lies in East Antarctica just to the east of the Transantarctic range.

West Antarctica is the much smaller region on the west side of the Transantarctic Mountains. West Antarctica includes a land feature called the Antarctic Peninsula. This is a narrow arm of land that extends more than 1,000 miles (1,600 kilometers) from the Antarctic land mass as if it were pointing toward South America.

Ice Shelves

Much of Antarctica's coastline is not land but ice. In many places, walls of ice extend from the actual coast some distance out into the ocean. These features are called ice shelves.

Natural barriers

Ice shelves float on the ocean and even move up and down a little as tides come in and go out. However, ice shelves are firmly attached to the land mass. Antarctica is the only place on Earth that has large, semipermanent ice shelves.

Vast ice shelves fill several of Antarctica's bays and channels.

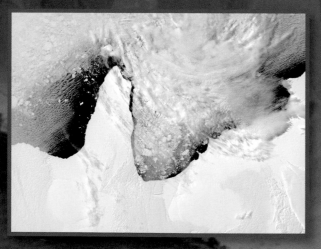 

Within a 24-hour period in 2010, an area of sea ice larger than the state of Rhode Island broke away from the Ronne-Filchner Ice Shelf in Antarctica. The detailed images were captured by NASA satellites.

Tourists experience the vastness of Antarctica's Ross Ice Shelf. Bigger than the state of California, the shelf is 2,300 feet (700 meters) thick bordering land and 660 feet (200 meters) thick bordering the ocean.

What's in a Name?

Scientists call the part of an ice shelf that joins it to solid land the hinge. They say that the ice shelf "hinges" when it rises and drops with the tide. This scientific term was inspired by the common hardware used on doors and some boxes with tops.

How ice shelves form

An ice shelf takes many years to form. Parts of the Antarctic **ice sheet** push slowly toward the coast from higher interior regions. Often, the end of a **glacier** will break off and form **icebergs** when it reaches the sea. However, sometimes it stays together and pushes farther and farther over water. In time, seawater underneath the glacial ice freezes to it. This process forms an ice shelf.

Some of the Antarctic ice shelves are huge. For example, the Ross Ice Shelf is slightly larger than the state of California. It is about 2,300 feet (700 meters) thick at its inner edge (against land) and about 660 feet (200 meters) thick at its outer edge (bordering the ocean). As with icebergs, much of the ice in an ice shelf is actually underwater.

When ice shelves break apart

Chunks of ice shelves can break off to form immense, flat icebergs called tabular icebergs. Since the early 1970's, when **satellites** became available, this process has been observed several times.

Antarctic Explorers

People first saw Antarctica in the 1800's. Serious exploration of the continent began after 1900.

Mysterious continent

For most of human history, people knew nothing of the frozen continent at the bottom of the world. Then in the 1820's, several explorers sailed close enough to see Antarctica. However, they probably did not realize they were looking at a huge land mass.

In 1895, Norwegian Henryk Johan Bull became the first person to step ashore on the Antarctic mainland. Bull was sailing on a ship used for hunting whales.

The race to the South Pole

In the early 1900's, two explorers made plans to lead **expeditions** to the South Pole. They were Robert F. Scott of the United Kingdom and Roald Amundsen of Norway. Such an expedition would not be easy. It would require training and conditioning as well as money for ships and supplies.

Scott made a first expedition to Antarctica between 1901 and 1904. With him was Ernest Shackleton, who led his own expedition in 1907.

In 1911, both Scott and Amundsen set out to Antarctica, determined to reach the South Pole. Newspapers around the world reported on their "race to the pole." Amundsen reached the South Pole on December 14, 1911. Scott's party arrived about a month later. Amundsen and his men returned to safety. Tragically, Scott's party became trapped in a blizzard and froze to death.

British Navy Captain Robert F. Scott, standing, became the first person to reach the South Polar plateau. However, explorer Roald Amundsen beat him to the true South Pole by five weeks.

Travel by plane

In 1929, U.S. Navy officer Richard E. Byrd became the first person to fly over the South Pole. With the help of airplanes and tractors, Byrd and his assistants made several expeditions to Antarctica in the 1930's and 1940's.

Women in Antarctica

In 1947, U.S. explorer Finn Ronne led a scientific expedition to Antarctica. With him were his wife, Edith Ronne, and the scientist Jenny Darlington. They were the first women to spend a winter in Antarctica.

Later exploration

In early 1958, British scientist Vivian Fuchs led a land expedition across the entire continent of Antarctica. The expedition started in the Weddell Sea to the east of the Antarctic Peninsula. It ended up at McMurdo Sound in the Ross Sea in western Antarctica.

In January 1997, Norwegian Borge Ousland became the first person to walk and ski across Antarctica alone. Ousland followed a route (path) similar to that of Fuchs. He covered 1,675 miles (2,700 kilometers), carrying all his supplies with him.

Antarctica's First Newspaper

During Robert Scott's first expedition to Antarctica in 1902, his assistant, Ernest Shackleton, "published" a newspaper called the *South Polar Times*. It was a short journal to entertain the crew during the long Antarctic winter. Camped on the Antarctic coast, Scott and his crew experienced four months of polar night. During this time, the men could do little but wait in their huts.

Roald Amundsen, standing next to the flag of Norway, reached the South Pole on December 14, 1911.

Is Antarctica a Country?

Antarctica has no permanent population and is not a country. The nations of the world have agreed to share it as a peaceful reserve for science.

Antarctica is a continent—but it is not a country. People have not lived on Antarctica as a permanent home. All the people in Antarctica are there on assignment for short-term scientific projects.

Early claims to the continent

As explorers began to visit Antarctica more than 100 years ago, they began to claim parts of Antarctica for their home countries. The first Antarctic explorers were from Norway and the United Kingdom, so those nations made early claims to pieces of Antarctic territory. The continent's distant neighbors—Chile and Argentina from the southern tip of South America and Australia and New Zealand—have also made claims to Antarctica.

Most other nations of the world do not recognize these claims. Although there is no clear agreement about who owns what, most of the world's nations have signed treaties that set aside Antarctica for peaceful purposes.

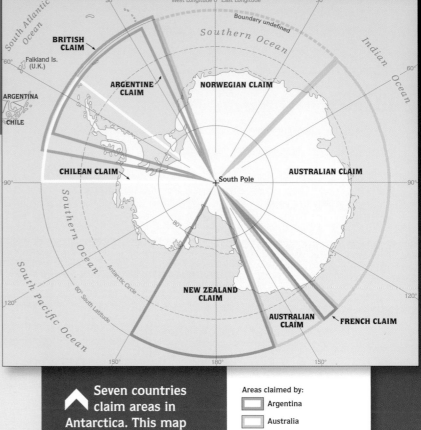

Seven countries claim areas in Antarctica. This map shows the boundaries of these areas, some of which overlap. The map also pinpoints major Antarctic research stations and indicates the country that operates each station.

Areas claimed by:
- Argentina
- Australia
- Chile
- France
- New Zealand
- Norway
- United Kingdom

0   1,000 Miles
0   1,000 Kilometers

Nikita Khrushchev

At the Same Time...

The Cold War between the United States and the Soviet Union was at its height in the late 1950's. But in the fall of 1959, the Soviet leader, Nikita Khrushchev, came to the United States for a visit. Many people hoped that relations between the two superpowers would thaw. Then in 1960, the Soviets shot down a U.S. spy plane over their territory in Russia. The Cold War continued into the 1980's.

The IGY and the Treaty of 1959

In 1957, most of the world's nations participated in the International Geophysical Year (IGY). The IGY brought together the world's best scientists to study Earth. A major part of this effort was devoted to exploration and research in Antarctica. Even the United States and the Soviet Union (now Russia), who were bitter enemies at the time, cooperated in the scientific research.

Out of IGY grew a new idea. Antarctica would be kept free of military bases. Instead, it would become a scientific laboratory open to all. This idea was given form in the Antarctic Treaty of 1959. That treaty banned nuclear weapons from Antarctica and encouraged scientific research there.

Other developments

Another treaty, adopted in 1991, bans mining and oil and gas exploration from Antarctica. This treaty is called the Madrid Protocol. It also sets down strict rules designed to protect the Antarctic environment.

Antarctica is the first major part of the world to be set aside by the people of the world for peaceful uses. Many countries have scientific stations there. In the past half century, scientific cooperation in Antarctica has advanced many branches of science.

A biologist observes an emperor penguin in Antarctica.

Living Things in Antarctica

Most of Antarctica is ice-covered and brutally cold. Almost no animals or plants live in the continent's interior. But the coastal areas of Antarctica and the seas around it are brimming with life.

Microbes

Tiny living organisms called microbes thrive in many places in Antarctica. **Algae** can grow on ice, making their own food from sunlight. Individual algae are too small to see. But together, they color the snow pink or green.

Plants

Scientists have discovered plantlike **lichens** growing on rocks in the high valleys of Antarctic mountains. These places have some of the most severe weather in all of Antarctica.

Few true plants grow in Antarctica. Some mosses grow on rocky coastal areas. Flowering plants grow only on the Antarctic Peninsula. This peninsula in western Antarctica is very cold. But it is slightly warmer than the rest of Antarctica, especially lands to the east.

Animal life

Very few animals can survive inside Antarctica for long. But animals are abundant in the seas around Antarctica. Many animals live along the icy coasts.

A snowfield in Antarctica is covered with red algae.

An orca mother and calf surface for air in McMurdo Sound, Antarctica.

Whales

Many kinds of whales swim in Antarctic waters. They hunt for **krill,** squid, and fish. Among them are sperm whales, fin whales, and the largest animal that has ever lived, the blue whale.

Penguins

Penguins are flightless birds that swim in the ocean. They feed mainly on krill, fish, and squid.

Penguins return to land to breed. In Antarctica, penguins form huge **colonie**s at certain times of the year. Some colonies have 100,000 birds or more. Emperor penguins are among the only animals that spend winter in Antarctica. Males eat no food for four months, huddling together for warmth. The harsh winter weather keeps hunting animals away from penguin eggs and chicks

Two emperor penguin parents stand with their chick. Emperor penguins breed and raise their chicks during the harsh Antarctic winter.

Seals

Seals live along the coasts of Antarctica. Seals swim in the sea to hunt for krill, crabs, and fish. They come ashore to breed and to give birth.

The leopard seal is a fierce animal that hunts penguins. It attacks penguins from below, grabbing them with its strong jaws and sharp teeth. Leopard seals have even attacked people, though such occurrences are rare.

Flying birds

Many kinds of flying birds spend time in Antarctica. It is safer for them to lay eggs and raise chicks there because there are few hunting animals. One bird that frequents Antarctica, the albatross, is among the largest of flying birds, with a wingspan of up to 11½ feet (3.5 meters). During the southern winter, most of Antarctica's birds return to warmer places.

Did You Know?

The emperor penguin can dive in the ocean to a depth of nearly 2,000 feet (600 meters). It can hold its breath for 20 minutes or more.

Scientific Stations

Antarctica is not a permanent home for anyone. However, scientists, pilots, and other support persons live in scientific stations there for periods of time. These people are all involved in scientific research.

Challenges

Housing for people in Antarctic research stations has to be specially constructed. It must be very well insulated. (Insulating a building involves putting materials inside walls, under roofs, and above floors to keep heat from seeping out.) Buildings must also be able to withstand high winds. Large storerooms are necessary to store food, water, and other necessities. Furthermore, all of the building materials must be brought from another continent, either by plane or ship.

McMurdo Station has Antarctica's largest community. About 1,000 people live there during the warmer months.

McMurdo Station

McMurdo Station, operated by the U.S. National Science Foundation, is Antarctica's largest "city." During the Antarctic summer, it houses as many as 1,000 people. About 250 people inhabit the station in winter. The station has more than 100 structures, a harbor, an airport, and a helicopter pad.

McMurdo is located on bare volcanic rock on Ross Island. Ross Island is on McMurdo Sound at the edge of the Ross Ice Shelf. It is where Robert F. Scott established the first camp in Antarctica in 1910.

The chief scientific lab at McMurdo is the Albert P. Crary Science and Engineering Center. It opened in 1991.

Did You Know?

The Crary Science and Engineering Center at McMurdo Station was named for Albert P. Crary (1911–1987). Crary became the first person to set foot both on the North and South poles. He worked near the North Pole in the 1950's and near the South Pole in the 1960's.

The U.S. South Pole Station

In January 2008, the National Science Foundation opened a new scientific station at the South Pole. Named the Amundsen-Scott South Pole Station, the structure was designed to replace an aging domed structure built in 1975 and used until 2008.

▲ The Amundsen-Scott South Pole Station sits on a shifting continental ice sheet about 9,000 feet (2,700 meters) thick.

The new station is constructed to last through many harsh Antarctic winters and to protect the people inside. The structure is specially insulated to keep people warm and save energy. It is built on stilts so that snow will blow underneath it rather than piling up on the side. Different parts of the structure are connected by flexible halls and tunnels. This is because the "ground"—actually the surface of the Antarctic **ice sheet**—moves over time.

The Amundsen-Scott Station can house and protect a summer population of 150. The maximum winter population is about 50.

Other stations

There are more than 40 permanent scientific stations in Antarctica and surrounding islands. Countries that maintain stations include Argentina, Australia, Brazil, Bulgaria, Chile, China, Finland, France, Germany, India, Italy, Japan, New Zealand, Norway, Poland, Russia, South Africa, South Korea, Spain, Ukraine, the United Kingdom, the United States, and Uruguay.

A Good Appetite

People living and working at the Amundsen-Scott South Pole Station need more calories to stay healthy than people in other places. It takes a lot of energy to keep steady body heat in a very cold **climate**. Diet plans for the workers include about 5,000 calories per day. This is 2,000 to 3,000 more calories per day than recommended by the U.S. government for young adults living in the United States.

Warming in Antarctica

Over the past 50 years, the Antarctic Peninsula has warmed up by about 5 degrees Fahrenheit (2.8 degrees Celsius). It is warming faster than any other part of Earth except the Arctic.

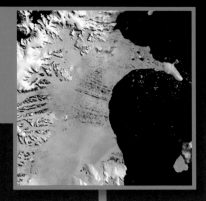

The warming west

The Antarctic Peninsula has been warming faster than other parts of our planet. The peninsula is especially sensitive to warming. In a 2005 study, researchers reported that 87 percent of **glaciers** on the coast of the peninsula are retreating. This retreat is speeding up over time. In 2002, most of the Larsen B **ice shelf** collapsed. In 2008, part of the Wilkins ice shelf collapsed. These two ice shelves are on opposite sides of the Antarctic Peninsula. The breakup of these ice shelves may speed the flow of ice into the sea.

While West Antarctica has been warming quickly, the temperature of East Antarctica has remained about the same. East Antarctica is high up, and strong winds protect it from the warm air of other regions. But most **climate** scientists warn that Antarctica is warming overall.

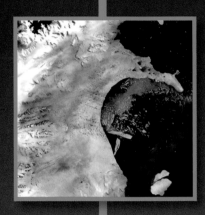

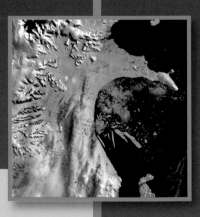

Satellite images show the breakup of the Larsen B ice shelf. The photographs were taken, from top to bottom, on January 31, 2002; February 17, 2002; February 23, 2002; and March 5, 2002. Antarctic ice shelves have been shrinking since at least the early 1970's because of warming in the region.

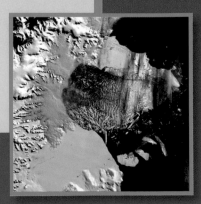

Change comes to the Antarctic region

A warming climate is changing Antarctica and the seas around it. For many living things in Antarctica, **global warming** could mean trouble.

Many Antarctic animals depend on shrimplike **krill** for food. During the winter, krill feed on **algae** under the sea ice. As the sea ice shrinks because of global warming, there are fewer krill. Fewer krill means fewer fish, penguins, seals, and other animals.

Even giant whales depend on tiny krill. For example, the blue whale is the largest animal that has ever lived. It reaches 100 feet (30 meters) long and weighs more than 150 tons (135 metric tons). Incredibly, it reaches this size eating nothing but krill.

Sadly, people hunted whales until many **species** almost died out completely. People killed more than 300,000 blue whales in Antarctic waters alone. Today, most whale hunting has been banned, and many species have begun to recover. But only about 3,000 blue whales remain in Antarctic waters. If global warming makes it hard for whales to find krill, many species might not recover. Blue whales could disappear forever.

Invasive species

As the Antarctic warms, plants and animals from other regions may invade the continent. In 2004, researchers studying the Antarctic Peninsula discovered that cushion plants and a type of grass had invaded the land. These plants did not grow on the peninsula as recently as 1995.

Such invasive species—living things that spread rapidly after they arrive in new areas—compete with native animals and plants. Many native animals plants are found nowhere but Antarctica. Invasive species could wipe them out forever.

Green Light for Glaciers

Scientists warn that the breakup of ice shelves in Antarctica could cause glaciers to speed up on their way to the sea. An ice shelf acts as a brake on the movement of the glaciers behind it on land. If an ice shelf breaks up, this brake is removed. The glaciers may then slide more rapidly into the sea. In fact, scientists have found that glaciers in Greenland and Antarctica are flowing more quickly. That will cause sea levels to rise faster.

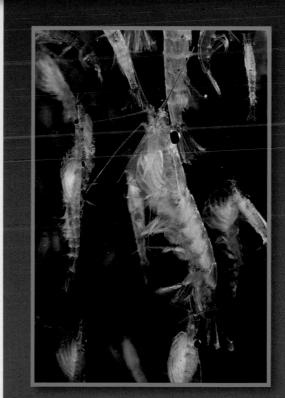

Many kinds of whales eat vast amounts of krill daily. Changes due to global warming could reduce krill populations and disrupt the Antarctic food chain.

Environmental Threats to Polar Regions

Development and global warming are changing the polar regions. Some of these changes could harm polar environments.

Resource-rich lands and seas

Polar regions are rich but fragile. They contain valuable animal and **mineral** resources. But these areas are easily damaged by human activities.

For centuries, people of the Arctic took only the resources they could use themselves. More recently, industry has taken resources on a larger scale. Boats have removed billions of fish from the sea. Energy companies have built pipelines across the **tundra.** When pipelines or oil tankers leak, the damage can be severe.

Fishing

In the last 100 years, fishing boats have become more advanced. Without careful management, modern fishing fleets can catch too many fish. The waters of the Arctic are some of the richest in the ocean. But some kinds of fish have been nearly wiped out by overfishing.

In the oceans around Antarctica, people have begun to fish for large amounts of shrimplike **krill.** These krill are made into fish feed and other products. However, many animals depend on krill for food. If too many krill are taken, some animals may not survive.

Commercial fishermen haul in a catch of salmon in Alaska.

▲ The *Exxon Valdez* oil spill dumped nearly 11 million gallons (42 million liters) of crude oil into Prince William Sound, part of the Gulf of Alaska. It killed thousands of animals, including about 250,000 birds.

The Killing Fields of Antarctica

The Antarctic fur seal is a **species** that breeds on islands in the Antarctic region. Around the year 1800, ships that specialize in hunting seals began visiting islands near Antarctica. There they found huge numbers of seals in rookeries (breeding grounds). They killed as many as they could take. By the end of the 1800's, they had hunted the seals nearly to extinction. Fortunately, populations of the seals recovered, and today Antarctic fur seals are protected by international agreements.

Did You Know?

Alaska's largest herd of caribou is called the Western Arctic Herd. In 2007, the Alaska Department of Fish and Game counted the herd. They found 377,000 caribou. That was 113,000 fewer caribou than were in the herd the last time they counted, in 2003.

Big oil comes to the Arctic

In 1977, U.S. oil companies completed the Trans-Alaska Pipeline from the northern Arctic coast of Alaska to its southern coast. The pipeline allowed oil companies to begin pumping oil out of Alaska's far Arctic north.

Oil has brought wealth to Alaska, but it has also caused problems. In March 1989, the *Exxon Valdez* oil tanker wrecked near Prince William Sound on Alaska's southern coast. It dumped nearly 11 million gallons (42 million liters) of oil into the sound.

There also have been problems with pipelines. In 2006, a smaller pipeline spilled more than 200,000 gallons (750,000 liters) of crude oil onto the tundra of northern Alaska. In 2009, another pipeline in the same area spilled 46,000 gallons (175,000 liters).

The Trans-Alaska Pipeline carries oil about 800 miles (1,300 kilometers), from Prudhoe Bay in northern Alaska to the port of Valdez on the state's southern coast.

Companies and countries are searching for new riches in the polar regions. Tapping these riches could harm polar environments.

Global warming creates new opportunities

As **global warming** reduces sea ice, many areas of the Arctic may open up to industry. In 2009, the U.S. Geological Survey announced that the Arctic may hold up to one-quarter of all the oil and natural gas on Earth. These riches have drawn the interest of energy companies. If global warming continues, these companies will likely explore Antarctica for **mineral** resources, too.

Greenland has issued licenses to energy companies to explore for oil and gas along the island's west coast. Energy companies hope to build oil platforms in the Beaufort Sea and Chukchi Sea, parts of the Arctic Ocean. Other efforts are moving ahead in the Arctic waters north of Russia.

However, environmentalists warn that oil exploration could damage beaches and pollute water. The Arctic is a cold and dangerous place to work. It is remote and difficult to reach. An accident could be devastating. Large oil spills have caused great damage to other areas. They would likely do even more damage to the fragile Arctic environment. Even worse, a large oil spill might be impossible to clean up in the Arctic because of the harsh conditions. That could mean years of environmental damage. A large Arctic oil spill could kill vast numbers of animals and change the lives of native peoples forever.

Oil rigs are floating platforms used to drill for oil or natural gas in the ocean. As sea ice continues to melt, drilling for such fossil fuels may increase in Arctic waters.

Precious minerals

Oil isn't the only substance that big companies could mine from the Arctic. In the early 2000's, an Australian mineral company found large deposits of rare earth metals near the southern tip of Greenland. Rare earth metals are a group of elements used in many electronics products. As of 2010, China produced about 95 percent of the world's supply of these minerals.

The company has received permission to start work on mining the rare earth metals. These minerals could bring much wealth to Greenland. However, environmentalists worry that mining in southern Greenland could do great damage to the fragile environment.

Minerals in Antarctica

Because so much of Antarctica is ice-covered, scientists do not know very much about its mineral resources. However, explorers have found coal and iron ore on the continent. Some scientists suspect that oil and gas reserves likely lie underneath the waters around Antarctica. These resources would be too difficult and expensive to mine today. However, that could change if global warming continues. Given the world's hunger for energy and minerals, industry may soon come to Antarctica.

Nearly all of Antarctica is ice-covered. However, if global warming causes melting, mining companies could become interested in exploring for mineral riches there.

Rare Earth Metals

Rare earth metals are a group of scarce chemical elements. Purifying them is expensive and produces toxic waste. Many of the machines and devices we depend on today could not function without rare earth metals. Here are some examples.

- Europium makes possible red color in televisions.

- Neodymium makes it possible to miniaturize powerful magnets that can be used in computers, cars, and other devices. It is also used to make parts of hybrid cars.

- Lanthanum is used in certain rechargeable batteries.

- Erbium and neodymium are used to make lasers.

Using—and Sharing—Earth's Icy Worlds

People are becoming more and more interested in the polar regions. But this interest is causing some tension among nations.

The world's hunger for energy

The world economy runs on energy. As the economy grows, the world needs more and more oil and natural gas. Taking oil and other **mineral** riches from the Arctic is risky. An accident in northern waters could do much damage. But the need for energy is great. The wealth to be made from such resources is incredible. As a result, companies and countries will likely move ahead with plans to collect those resources. That raises another question: Who exactly owns the Arctic?

Competition—and tension

As northern countries look to the Arctic for mineral riches, they come into conflict. Each country that borders the Arctic Ocean owns some ocean extending from its shorelines. However, most of the Arctic Ocean does not have clear boundaries. Countries disagree about who controls different parts of the Arctic.

The nations of the Arctic will have to work out agreements about who owns what before companies begin taking such resources as oil out of the Arctic Ocean. In September 2010, representatives of Canada, Denmark (representing Greenland), Norway, Russia, and the United States met in Moscow. They discussed their territorial claims in the Arctic. No agreements were made, but the countries did agree to keep talking.

Emperor penguins make their way across the ice on Snow Hill Island, Antarctica, as a group of curious tourists looks on.

Tourists cruise by a gigantic **glacier** in Paradise Bay, Alaska. Ecotourism may raise awareness about threats to polar regions.

Planting Flags

In August 2007, Russian explorers planted their country's flag on the floor of the Arctic Ocean underneath the North Pole. The explorers, using three-person submarines, drove the flagpole into the seabed approximately 14,000 feet (4,200 meters) under the Arctic sea ice. The flag was made of titanium, a metal that does not rust.

For the world's people

In a sense, natural beauty belongs to all the world's people. There was a time when only scientists and soldiers visited polar regions. Now, an increasing number of ordinary people visit the ends of the earth. Visitors who come to view natural beauty and learn about the environment are called ecotourists.

Special travel companies offer ecotours to the Arctic and Antarctica. For example, people can take airplane trips to the North Pole. Some companies offer rugged travel on skis and dogsleds led by experienced guides. Others offer more comfortable methods of travel, such as cruises on luxurious ships. Ships travel to the waters around Antarctica. Side **expeditions** even allow tourists to briefly set foot on the Antarctic continent.

Ecotourists with High Aims

In December 1996, six mountain climbers led by photographer Gordon Wiltsie went to Queen Maud Land, Antarctica, to climb a knife-edged mountain peak. The peak, called "The Razor," is a shaft of solid rock rising 2,000 feet (610 meters) above the **ice sheet**. The climbers reached the top of the peak on January 3, 1997, and beheld a majestic view never before seen by people.

Windows into the Past

Ice cores and fossils tell scientists much about the distant past of the Arctic and Antarctica. These regions were not always icy worlds.

Scientists study the **ice sheets** of Greenland and Antarctica. The many layers of ice tell them much about the history of the polar regions— and of the whole Earth.

Cycles of change

The polar regions have changed many times over Earth's long history. For example, Greenland did not have an ice sheet 3 million years ago. More than 30 million years ago, Antarctica was ice-free, too.

Ice cores

One of the best tools that scientists have to study the polar ice sheets are ice cores. An ice core is a long, narrow tube of ice taken from a **glacier** or ice sheet. Scientists insert a special instrument into the ice surface and drive it deeply down to take out an ice core.

The ice in a glacier has many layers. The layers correspond to year after year of snowfall as the glacier formed. From these layers, scientists can determine when different parts of the glacier were laid down.

A researcher inspects an ice core drilled from a glacier at the Mount Redoubt volcano summit crater in Alaska.

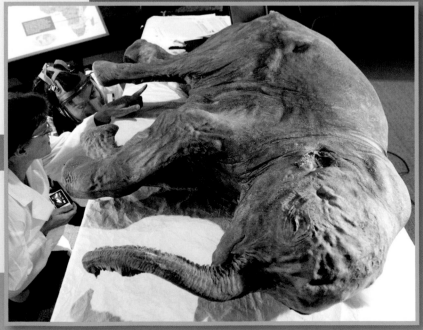

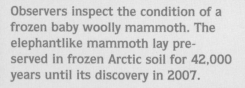

Observers inspect the condition of a frozen baby woolly mammoth. The elephantlike mammoth lay preserved in frozen Arctic soil for 42,000 years until its discovery in 2007.

Ice bubbles

Light, fluffy snow traps much air as it covers the ground. When snow in a glacier becomes pressed into glacial ice, this air forms bubbles in the ice. These bubbles are like time capsules. They reveal what Earth's **atmosphere** was like in the past.

Ice cores taken from the ice sheet in Antarctica offer important clues about **global warming** today. These cores show that there is more carbon dioxide and methane in our atmosphere today than for 650,000 years past. (Carbon dioxide and methane are both **greenhouse gases** that trap heat in Earth's atmosphere.) This finding is one of many pieces of evidence that the build-up of greenhouse gases is causing global warming.

Fossils

Fossils are the preserved remains of organisms from very long ago. The types of plants and animals preserved in fossils tell us much about the conditions of the distant time in which they lived.

Fossils found in Antarctica show that it was once a much warmer place than today. Fossil leaves and wood prove that large, sturdy plants once thrived in Antarctica. Scientists have even found the remains of dinosaurs in rocky mountainsides.

About 100 million years ago, Earth's continents were not positioned as they are today. Over time, the continents have moved. In the age of the dinosaurs, Antarctica was probably connected to or very close to Australia. And it was much warmer.

What's in a Name?

In 1991, a team of scientists found dinosaur bones on a rocky Antarctic mountainside. They named the newly discovered **species** *Cryolophosaurus ellioti*. *Cryolophosaurus* means "cold crested lizard." (A crest is a bony ridge on the top of some dinosaurs' heads.) *Ellioti* honors David Elliot, the scientist who found the first bones of the fossil.

Cryolophosaurus ellioti

Ice on Other Worlds

In November 2009, researchers in Antarctica drilled a hole in the Ross Ice Shelf and lowered a video camera. The hole, 600 feet (180 meters) deep, allowed the camera to take pictures of the seawater underneath the shelf.

To the researchers' amazement, they found a 3-inch (7-centimeter) shrimplike animal swimming in the water. The hole was 12 miles (19 kilometers) from open ocean. The shrimplike animal could have drifted there, but the scientists did not expect to find it in such a dark, cold, barren place.

This discovery caused scientists to wonder if life could thrive on other icy worlds where similar conditions exist.

Jupiter's moon, Europa

The giant planet Jupiter has more than 60 moons. Among the largest of these is Europa. Europa has a very interesting surface that looks like ice that has formed on a puddle after a cold night. Scientists think that there is a vast, watery ocean underneath Europa's skin of ice. Some scientists believe that Europa's ice-cloaked ocean is one place in the solar system where life may have developed. They believe conditions there may be similar to those on the underside of large **ice shelves** in Antarctica.

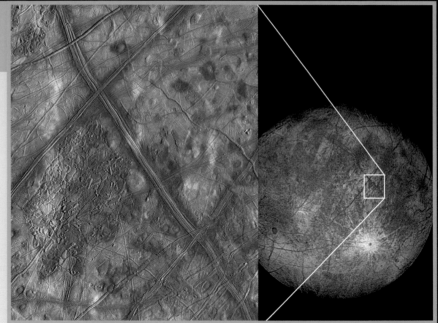

In this false-color image and inset (left), icy regions of Europa are shown in blue. Reddish-brown and white areas represent non-ice material.

Did You Know?

Water isn't the only substance that forms ice when chilled. For example, much of the ice on Saturn's moon Titan is ammonia ice rather than water ice. On Mars, carbon dioxide sometimes freezes and forms frost on the planet's surface.

Mars

The planet Mars has polar icecaps. Spacecraft sent to Mars have also found water ice in the soil underneath the planet's surface. Scientists have found evidence that Mars once had large amounts of liquid water. They believe that the **climate** changed on Mars millions of years ago. Nearly all of the water we see near the surface is ice.

Comets and asteroids

A comet is a ball of ice and dust that orbits (travels around) the sun. As the comet approaches the sun, it heats up and gives off gases. These gases form a "tail" on the comet. Scientists believe that most of the ice in a comet is water ice.

In 2010, scientists reported having used a special telescope to find water ice on an asteroid called 24 Themis. (An asteroid is a rocky object that is much smaller than a planet.) Previously, scientists had thought that asteroids were dry, iceless objects.

The moon

Many scientists thought that the moon was a bone-dry place. But in 2009, a U.S. **satellite** found evidence of water ice near the moon's south pole. Scientists think that the ice may have come from comets.

Ice among the stars

Water exists throughout the universe. Undoubtedly, our galaxy (system of stars, gas, dust, and other matter) holds many icy worlds. Perhaps someday, people will explore spectacular icy worlds around distant stars.

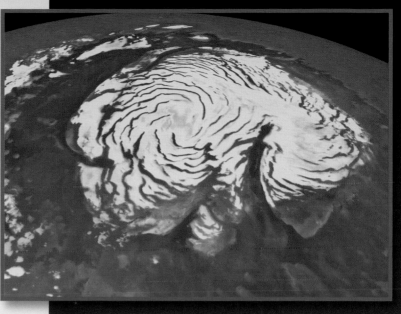

A satellite image shows the ice-covered north polar region of Mars.

Saturn's rings consist mainly of pieces of ice, which can be up to 10 feet (3 meters) in diameter.

Glossary

adapt   to make fit or suitable for a living thing's environment.

alga (plural: **algae**)   a water organism that uses sunlight to make food. Seaweeds are algae.

artificial satellite   a human-made object that continuously orbits Earth or some other body in space.

atmosphere   the blanket of air surrounding Earth.

axis   an imaginary line through the center of a globe.

bog   a piece of soft, wet, spongy ground. A bog consists chiefly of decayed or decaying moss and other vegetable matter.

climate   the weather that occurs at a particular place over a long period of time.

colony   a group of animals of the same kind living together.

expedition   a journey made for some special purpose.

geologist   a scientist who studies rocks and soil.

glacier   a large mass of ice formed from snow on high ground and moving very slowly down a mountain or along a sloping valley, or spreading slowly over a large area of land until it melts or breaks up.

global warming   The increase in average temperatures around the world over the last 200 years.

greenhouse gas   a gas that traps heat in Earth's atmosphere; examples include carbon dioxide and methane.

iceberg   a huge, floating chunk of ice in the ocean.

ice floe   a floating piece of sea ice.

ice sheet   a glacier that forms on relatively flat land and spreads over a very wide area.

ice shelf   a mass of coastal ice that is attached to land but also floats on the ocean and experiences tides.

krill   a small, shrimplike animal that exists in huge floating populations in oceans throughout the world.

lichen   a plantlike organism that consists of algae and fungi living together.

mineral   a solid, natural substance that is not a plant or animal, and which was never alive.

permafrost   ground that is deeply frozen most or all of the time.

precipitation   forms of water falling from the sky, such as rain, snow, sleet, or hail.

satellite   see *artificial satellite.*

species   a group of living things with similar characteristics. Animals of the same species can breed with one another.

temperate region   a region of Earth that has seasons of hot and cold; the area between equatorial and polar regions.

tundra   treeless areas in very cold places, such as the Arctic region and some high mountains.

Find Out More

Books

Antarctica: Journeys to the South Pole by Walter Dean Myers (Scholastic Press, 2004)

An Arctic Ecosystem by Greg Roza (PowerKids Press, 2009)

Frozen Secrets: Antarctica Revealed by Sally M. Walker (Carolrhoda Books, 2010)

Polar Explorations: Journeys to the Arctic and the Antarctic by Martyn Bramwell and others (DK Publishers, 1998)

Searching for Arctic Oil by Eve Hartman and Wendy Meschbesher (Raintree, 2011)

Survivor's Science in the Polar Regions by Peter D. Riley (Raintree, 2005)

Tundra by Peter D. Moore and Richard Garratt (Chelsea House, 2006)

Websites

Arctic Change
http://www.arctic.noaa.gov/detect/

This site, from the National Oceanic and Atmospheric Administration (NOAA), features information on climate change and the many ecosystems of the Arctic. It also includes the Arctic Report Card, an annual update on the Arctic environment.

Arctic: A Friend Acting Strangely
http://forces.si.edu/arctic/index.html

Part of the Forces of Change exhibition, this site offers eyewitness views of climate change from scientists and Arctic residents alike. Includes a documentary video.

Arctic Studies Center
http://www.mnh.si.edu/arctic

The National Museum of Natural History at the Smithsonian Institution maintains this site, which is full of information on the people and cultures of Alaska and the Arctic.

Australian Antarctic Division
http://www.antarctica.gov.au/

This website, provided by Australia's Antarctic Program, has information about each of Australia's Antarctic research stations, as well as current science news and a glimpse into the life of an Antarctic researcher.

Freeze Frame: Historic Polar Images
http://www.freezeframe.ac.uk/home/home

A gallery of images illustrating the history of Arctic and Antarctic exploration, maintained by the Scott Polar Research Institute.

In the Spotlight: What Is Antarctica?
http://www.nasa.gov/audience/forstudents/
5-8/features/what-is-antarctica-58.html

This site is a look at NASA's work in (and above) the world's coldest continent.

NASA LIMA: Faces of Antarctica
http://lima.nasa.gov/

The Landsat Image Mosaic of Antarctica (LIMA) uses satellite technology to show the world what Antarctica really looks like. The site includes a video flying tour of the McMurdo Station.

Polar Regions: The Ends of the Earth
http://wwf.panda.org/about_our_earth/ecoregions/about/habitat_types/habitats/polar_regions/

Learn about the different kinds of animals that thrive in the polar regions and the tundra.

Race to the End of the Earth
http://www.amnh.org/exhibitions/race/

Follow the paths of explorers Roald Amundsen and Robert Falcon Scott as they race each other to the South Pole in 1910.

Special Report: U.S. South Pole Station
http://www.nsf.gov/news/special_reports/
livingsouthpole/intro.jsp

Tour the Amundsen-Scott South Pole Station, both past and present, and read about the goals and projects of the scientists who live and work there.

Index